The Audacious Little Duck
(Bubble in Trouble)
A Lesson Of Danger

Liliane Boctor

Copyright © 2018 by Liliane Boctor.

All rights reserved. No part of this publication may be reproduced, distributed, or transmitted in any form or by any means, including photocopying, recording, or other electronic or mechanical methods, without the prior written permission of the author, except in the case of brief quotations embodied in critical reviews and certain other noncommercial uses permitted by copyright law.

Printed in the United States of America
ISBN: 978-1-64460-142-6 (Paperback)
ISBN: 978-1-64460-143-3 (Ebook)
ISBN: 978-1-64460-141-9 (Hardback)
Library of Congress Control Number: 2019940142

Stonewall Press
363 Paladium Court
Owings Mills, MD 21117
www.stonewallpress.com
1-888-334-0980

This is dedicated to my grandchildren, Holden, Sebastien, Brittany and Carter, who give joy and meaning to my life. It is difficult to find words to express how much I love you all.

TWINKLE the warbler of the reeds has followed BUBBLE the little yellow duck throughout his journey without letting him know of her presence. She enters the cave after him, and wonders where the GIGANTIC FROG is. The underground cave is very humid, and water is dripping from the top center of the cave, which makes it very slippery.

BUBBLE the little yellow duck slowly approaches, when suddenly, a deep thundering voice says to him,

"WHAT?"

Looking around BUBBLE is trying to determine from what area of the cave the voice is coming from.

"WHAT?" says the voice once again.

BUBBLE trembles and answers, "NOTHING!"

The deep voice replies, "HOW NOTHING?"

BUBBLE the little yellow duck is terrified by the voice.

"When once enters, one introduces himself in my home! When I ask "WHAT?" I expect an answer – BUT NOTHING! Come here so I can see you better!" says LEONA THE GIGANTIC FROG.

"Who are you? And what are you doing here?" asks LEONA THE GIGANTIC FROG. With fear, and carefully, BUBBLE the little yellow duck takes four steps forward, and freezes. Staring back at him is the most enormous, extraordinary frog that he has ever laid eyes on. The frog has eyes as big as saucers.

BUBBLE the little yellow duck answers with a weak voice, "Madame the QUEEN, I hope I am addressing you properly! I do not want to offend you! My name is BUBBLE, and I travel throughout the region to educate myself! It's by coincidence that our paths have crossed while I am pursuing some worms for dinner!" says BUBBLE to LEONA the GIGANTIC FROG.

"It's never my intention to upset you by entering your beautiful palace!" says BUBBLE the little yellow duck to LEONA the GIGANTIC FROG.

"When you said to me, "What?", I answered "nothing!" because I really did not have anything to say." says BUBBLE.

BUBBLE the little yellow duck is scared, VERY SCARED! He tremble with fear, and makes sure not to look at LEONA'S the GIGANTIC FROG eyes. He remembers the stories OSCAR the raccoon told him about those who have disappeared when searching for the magical necklace.

Her Majesty LEONA THE GIGANTIC FROG replied, "Huh! Huh! Personally I do not have lots of confidence in our situation. Approach! Approach! So I can see you better, and if you behave I will let you leave, only if you've sworn not to tell anyone what you saw." she says to BUBBLE the little yellow duck.

TWINKLE the warbler of the reeds is worried, and she wonders what LEONA THE GIGANTIC FROG is going to do to BUBBLE the little yellow duck. Right away, she begins to inspect the premises.

Suddenly, TWINKLE discovers a small hole between a few rocks.

The hole is large enough for her to go in and out of the horrible cave. She feels joy at having another escape route in the event that something goes wrong.

Terrified, after a few moments, BUBBLE the little yellow duck regains his courage, realizing that the dangerous LEONA THE GIGANTIC FROG cannot read his thoughts and is completely incapable of guessing his own motive. BUBBLE starts to waddle freely around the cave, inspecting all there is to see. His goal is to discover the hiding place of the magical necklace.

Unfortunately, BUBBLE the little yellow duck doesn't see the necklace, nor does he find anything resembling a hiding place. There are no markings, no secret doors or passageways.

Disappointed, BUBBLE wonders where the magic necklace is hidden, and why the other folks disappeared.

Then **LEONA THE GIGANTIC FROG** says, "You can rest here, against the wall! But do not move far away from me! I want to see you at all times. And I am sure you won't run away before tomorrow morning when you have to take the oath. Just remember, I sleep with one eye open!" she says to **BUBBLE** the little yellow duck

"Goodnight!" says **LEONA**.

BUBBLE the little yellow duck snuggles in the corner that is assigned to him, while LEONA THE GIGANTIC FROG crouches down a little more to take a rest... All of a sudden, right behind the head of LEONA as she bends down, BUBBLE catches sight of a nest that is built into a recessed area of the rock. In the nest sits the most beautiful necklace with multi-colored reflections.

It is overwhelming! BUBBLE the little yellow duck is so shocked by his observation that he almost screams.

Immediately, he calms himself down so that LEONA THE GIGANTIC FROG will not be alarmed in any way. BUBBLE knows he must be cautious. One kick of LEONA'S leg it will be over and his fate will be sealed. So he spends the whole night thinking. "How can I escape from this horrible cave?" BUBBLE wonders.

By the time morning comes in, BUBBLE the little yellow duck has a plan in the event that LEONA THE GIGANTIC FROG changes her mind. After he swears not to speak of his visit to anyone, BUBBLE is hoping LEONA will let him go home, but she decides to keep him longer. BUBBLE realizes he has to put his plan to work otherwise he will never see his brothers, mother and friends again.

BUBBLE the little yellow duck decides to walk around the premises, and when he approaches the stairs made of moist clay, he utters a scream, and cries, "Oh! Oh!"

Immediately thereafter, **BUBBLE** feels the soil tremble from the vibration of the sound, and promptly hears a thundering "What?"

Drawn by her curiosity, **LEONA THE GIGANTIC FROG** approaches. As she takes her first step going down the stairs, she slips on the moist clay and tries to keep herself steady, but driven by her weight, trying to hold on, **LEONA** slip and falls on her back. She is stuck right in the entryway.

LEONA THE GIGANTIC FROG makes every effort to dig herself out, but is unable to. She moans and moans with a terrifying voice. **LEONA is immobilized!**

Now feeling assured that LEONA is not able to stand up or move, BUBBLE the little yellow duck dashes toward the nest and takes possession of the magical necklace, and places it on his neck.

After a while BUBBLE the little yellow duck realizes that he forgot to plan his escape route. "Oh dear! LEONA THE GIGANTIC FROG is blocking the entryway of the underground cave. What to do?" BUBBLE wonders. The plan that has succeeded so well and appeared so ingenious seems to serve at nothing. "I am in possession of the magical necklace, and I cannot leave the horrible cave."

"What should I do!" BUBBLE the little yellow duck wonders. "I will never benefit from its treasures, and never be able to see my family and friends again. I am condemned to die in this obscure underground cave with LEONA THE GIGANTIC FROG."

After entertaining this thought, courageous BUBBLE the little yellow duck feels so small and sad that he starts to cry. Tears roll down his beak.

TO BE CONTINUED

www.ingramcontent.com/pod-product-compliance
Lightning Source LLC
Chambersburg PA
CBHW041153070526